My Mummy's an AVIATOR

My Mummy is an Aviator
Copyright © 2024 by Angel Pie Publishing

All rights reserved.

No part of this publication may be reproduced, distributed, or transmitted in any form or by any means, including photocopying, recording, or other electronic or mechanical methods, without the prior written permission of the publisher, except as permitted by U.S.A & U.K. copyright law. For permission requests, contact Angel Pie Publishing via TalulaGrey.com.

The story, all names, characters, and incidents portrayed in this production are fictitious. No identification with actual persons (living or deceased), places, buildings, and products is intended or should be inferred.

ISBN 978-1-0683134-0-0

This book belongs to...

How to Enjoy This Story

This book is written in a free-form style, without strict rhyme or rhythm, to reflect real-life experiences. Each page explores a different role within the Airforce, helping children understand why these jobs matter, why helping others is so important, and why sometimes parents must be far from home.

The story is designed to grow with your child, sparking conversations about family, bravery, and the many important roles in the Airforce. Here are some tips on how to make the most of it with children of different ages.

For Children Under 3

•   Explore Together: Focus on the illustrations, describing what you see. Point out people, creatures, uniforms, equipment, and places in simple words.

•   Story Moments: Share short sentences or phrases like, "Mummy/Daddy helps the planes fly" or "These friends keep people safe." Let your child point to things they notice or find interesting.

For Children 3-5 Years Old

- Read Aloud: Read the story aloud, pausing to explain words and ideas. Use the pictures to help explain terms like "mission," "humanitarian aid," or "natural disaster."
- Ask Questions: Encourage curiosity by asking questions like, "What do you think this person does?" or "Where do you think this helicopter is going?" This helps build understanding in an interactive way.

For Children 6 and Older

- Encourage Reading Together: Invite your child to read along with you or try reading parts of the story themselves. Let them explore the detailed illustrations to discover the roles and missions in the Airforce.
- Discuss and Share: Talk about the different roles and why they're important. You might say, "Mummy/Daddy helps keep people safe," or "This is a special job that helps everyone work together." Let your child ask questions, and use the book as a chance to discuss your family's connection to the Airforce.

This book is an invitation to explore, imagine, and connect. Each page introduces a new role in the Airforce and tells part of the story of helping others, serving the country, and acting with honour. Through their own sacrifice of having a parent away, military children, too, serve with honour and courage.

However you use it, I hope this story becomes a treasured part of your child's understanding of the Airforce, the value of service, and the important role their family plays.

My mummy's away on an operation,
For six months in a foreign location.
She's an aviator in the Royal Air Force,
Using air power to protect us all.
Mummy's been sent on an important mission,
To show off our might and represent the United Kingdom.

The RAF, established in nineteen eighteen,
Was the first independent air force the world had seen.
They have pilots to fly their aircraft high,
Like helicopters and jets soaring in the sky.
Engineers, medical staff, chefs, and whole
Teams of computer experts and air traffic control.

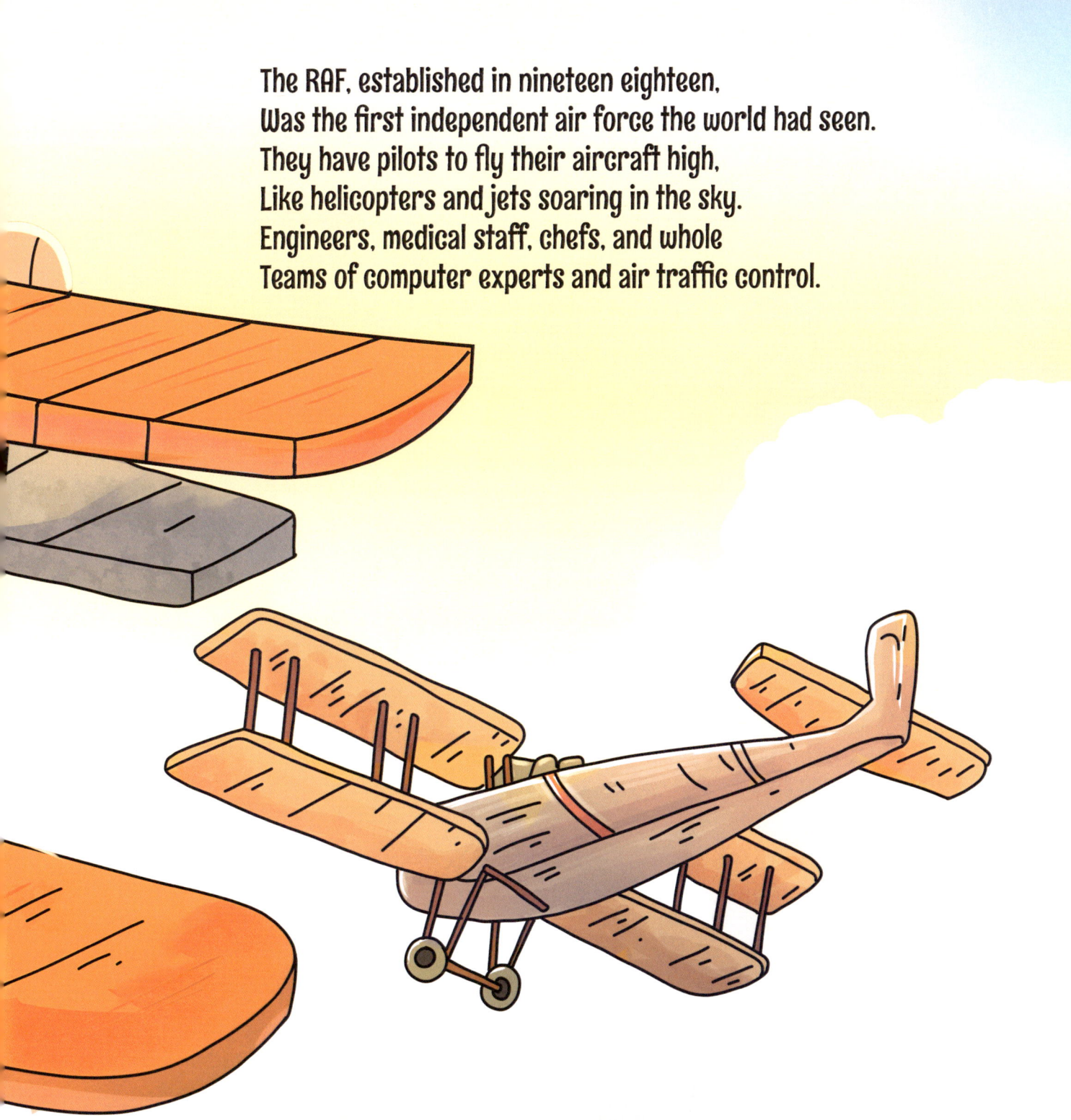

My mummy's a hero, saving people in need,
Delivering food and medical supplies with speed.
From disasters like hurricanes and tidal waves,
Helicopters evacuate those who need to be saved.
The Royal Air Force never fails,
When it comes to delivering humanitarian aid.

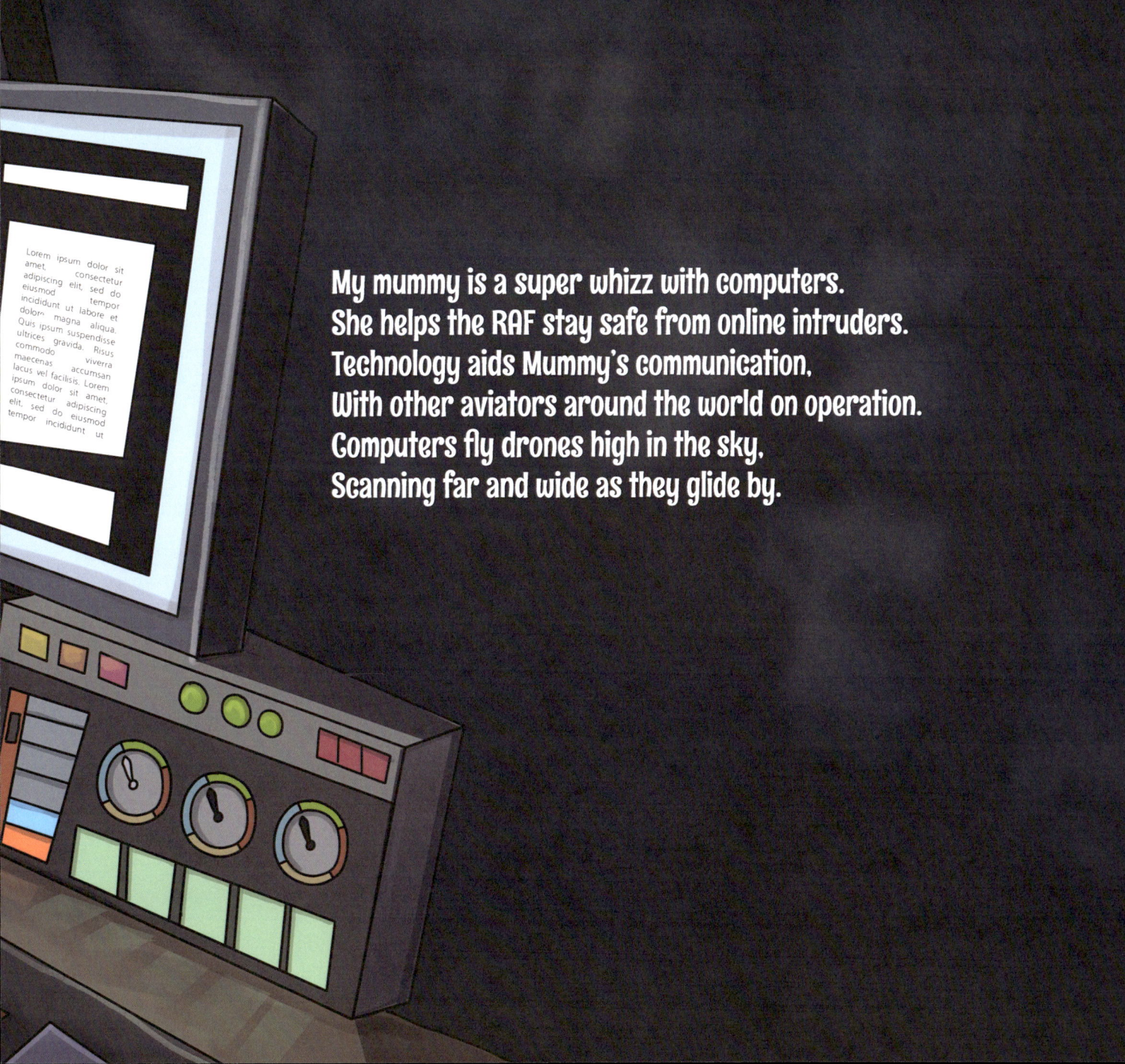

My mummy is a super whizz with computers.
She helps the RAF stay safe from online intruders.
Technology aids Mummy's communication,
With other aviators around the world on operation.
Computers fly drones high in the sky,
Scanning far and wide as they glide by.

My mummy works for a world of peace,
Reinforcing ties between nations to increase
Understanding of cultures far and wide,
Helping them work together, side by side.
The RAF gives training to distant nations,
Fostering peace for future generations.

UK Space Command is exciting and new,
Supporting rocket launches from England, it's true,
To help with communication both near and far,
RAF satellites float through space like a star!
An incredible feat of human engineering,
UK Space Command is truly pioneering.

The Red Arrows are the RAF's display team,
Thrilling crowds with dynamic and supreme
Manoeuvres, dazzling us with flips and dives,
With speed and grace, they soar through the sky.
With a trail of smoke of red, blue and white,
The jets thunder past at the speed of light.

On operations, there's no need to worry about Mummy getting lonely.
She's with her squadron on a base, the accommodation is quite homely.
With photos of me and our whole family on her wall,
She lays in her bed at night and thinks of us all.
There are gyms and restaurants available on the base.
There's even Wi-Fi so we can chat face to face.

Our family gets sad, doing everything without Mum is a struggle,
But I help with chores and give lots of cuddles.
We all miss Mummy but have friends who understand.
They're RAF families too and are around to lend a hand.
I have friends at school who are in the same situation,
They miss their parent too, who are away on operation.

I find it so hard when Mummy's away.
I miss her so much and count down the days.
Mum got a wall chart for me to tick
Each day as it passes, hoping it's quick.
Waiting for her to complete her mission and then
Return home to us, and the sky will be blue again.

I have a sweet jar and each sweet represents
Each day Mummy is away from the day she first went.
Every day I take one sweet savouring its taste.
But for me, it's much sweeter as it's another day faced.
When the day comes that the sweet jar is empty,
I know Mummy's coming home, there'll be celebrations aplenty.

When the sweet jar is empty and the wall chart is done,
I'll be so excited because my mummy's on her way home.
I miss Mummy when she's gone, I can't deny.
But like my mummy, I'm brave in stormy skies.
At bedtime, I look up at the sky and feel safe,
Proud to have a mummy who's an aviator in the RAF.

Talula Grey

Talula Grey is a navy wife, business owner, and writer of 'Daddy's at Sea' which was published on Amazon earlier this year. 'Mummy's at Sea' is the second book by Talula Grey and is the result of demand from mummy sailors, requesting a book that their children can relate to.

First and foremost, Talula is a mummy to her young son, a dog, a cat, and some fish. Talula has been married to her sailor husband for 7 years and enjoys the navy life; the lows are challenging, but they make the highs so much more exciting.

www.ingramcontent.com/pod-product-compliance
Lightning Source LLC
Chambersburg PA
CBRC090838010526
44118CB00007B/242